G.W.

Navigating the Storm

Strategies for Coping with Anxiety

This book was professionally typeset on Reedsy.
Find out more at reedsy.com

"Sometimes the most important thing in
a whole day is the rest taken between two
deep breaths."

— Etty Hillesum

Contents

1

Introduction

As I sat in the crowded café, surrounded by the comforting hum of conversation and the aroma of freshly brewed coffee, I couldn't shake the tightening grip of anxiety that seemed to suffocate me. It wasn't the noise or the crowd that bothered me; it was the irrational fear that gripped my chest, making it hard to breathe, and the relentless worry that seemed to consume my thoughts.

As I watched people around me chatting effortlessly, I envied their ease and wondered why I couldn't just be like them. Why did simple tasks like ordering a coffee or striking up a conversation feel like insurmountable challenges for me? Anxiety had become an unwelcome companion, lurking in the shadows of my mind and hijacking even the most mundane moments of my life.

It was this constant battle with anxiety that led me to embark on a journey of self-discovery and healing. I realized that I wasn't alone in my struggles and that there were countless others grappling with similar feelings of fear and uncertainty. It was this realization that inspired me to write this book – a guide to navigating the tumultuous waters of

1

anxiety with compassion, courage, and resilience.

Whether you're grappling with the crippling grip of panic attacks, the relentless chatter of worry, or the paralyzing fear of social interactions, this book is a beacon of light in the darkness. Together, we'll explore the intricate workings of anxiety, unravel its tangled knots, and forge a path towards healing and wholeness.

So, if you're tired of letting anxiety dictate your life and ready to embark on a journey of self-discovery and transformation, I invite you to join me on this adventure. Together, we'll uncover the strength within and discover that even in the midst of chaos, there is always room for calm.

2

Understanding Anxiety

nxiety and its various forms (generalized anxiety disorder, social anxiety, panic disorder, etc.)

Anxiety is a natural response to stress or perceived threats, characterized by feelings of apprehension, worry, or fear. While it's normal to experience occasional anxiety in response to stressful situations, anxiety becomes a disorder when it persists over time, interferes with daily life, and disrupts functioning.

Here are some common forms of anxiety disorders:

Generalized Anxiety Disorder (GAD): This is characterized by excessive, persistent worry and anxiety about a wide range of everyday events or activities. Individuals with GAD often find it difficult to control their worries, which can manifest as physical symptoms such as muscle tension, fatigue, irritability, and difficulty concentrating.

Social Anxiety Disorder (Social Phobia): Social anxiety disorder is marked by an intense fear of social situations or performance situations where the individual may be scrutinized or judged by others. This fear can lead to avoidance of social interactions, which can significantly impact personal and professional relationships. Physical symptoms such as sweating, trembling, and rapid heartbeat may accompany social anxiety.

Panic Disorder: Panic disorder involves recurrent, unexpected panic attacks characterized by sudden feelings of intense fear or discomfort. These panic attacks can be accompanied by physical symptoms such as chest pain, shortness of breath, dizziness, and feelings of impending doom. Individuals with panic disorder often live in fear of experiencing another panic attack and may avoid situations or places where they fear an attack might occur.

Specific Phobias: Specific phobias involve an intense, irrational fear of a particular object, situation, or activity. Common phobias include fear of heights (acrophobia), fear of flying (aviophobia), fear of spiders (arachnophobia), and fear of enclosed spaces (claustrophobia). When confronted with their phobia, individuals may experience intense anxiety and may go to great lengths to avoid the feared object or situation.

Obsessive-Compulsive Disorder (OCD): OCD is characterized by the presence of obsessions (persistent, intrusive thoughts or urges) and/or compulsions (repetitive behaviors or mental acts performed in response to obsessions). Common obsessions include fears of contamination, doubts about safety, and intrusive thoughts about harm. Compulsions are often performed in an attempt to reduce anxiety or prevent a feared outcome but provide only temporary relief.

Post-Traumatic Stress Disorder (PTSD): PTSD can develop after exposure to a traumatic event, such as combat, natural disasters, or physical or sexual assault. Symptoms may include intrusive memories or flashbacks of the traumatic event, avoidance of reminders of the event, negative changes in mood and cognition, and heightened arousal and reactivity.

These are just a few examples of anxiety disorders, and it's important to note that each individual may experience anxiety differently.

Seeking professional help from a mental health professional is crucial for accurate diagnosis and effective treatment.

The causes and triggers of anxiety, including genetic, environmental, and psychological factors.

Anxiety disorders can arise from a complex interplay of *genetic, environmental, and psychological factors*. Understanding these causes and triggers can provide insight into why some individuals are more susceptible to anxiety than others.

Genetic Factors

- Genetics play a significant role in predisposing individuals to anxiety disorders. Research suggests that there is a genetic component to anxiety, meaning that individuals with a family history of anxiety disorders are at a higher risk of developing one themselves.
- Specific genetic variations may contribute to differences in how individuals regulate neurotransmitters (chemical messengers in the brain), such as serotonin, dopamine, and gamma-aminobutyric

acid (GABA), which are involved in mood regulation and the stress response.

Environmental Factors

- Early life experiences, such as childhood trauma, neglect, or abuse, can significantly impact an individual's risk of developing anxiety disorders later in life. Adverse childhood experiences (ACEs) can disrupt the development of coping mechanisms and increase sensitivity to stress.
- Environmental stressors, such as financial difficulties, relationship problems, work or academic pressure, and major life changes (e.g., moving, divorce, loss of a loved one), can trigger or exacerbate anxiety symptoms in susceptible individuals.
- Chronic exposure to stressful or traumatic events, such as natural disasters, accidents, or violence, can also contribute to the development of anxiety disorders, particularly post-traumatic stress disorder (PTSD).

Psychological Factors

- Personality traits and temperament may influence an individual's vulnerability to anxiety. For example, individuals who are naturally more cautious, sensitive, or perfectionistic may be more prone to developing anxiety disorders.
- Cognitive factors, such as negative thought patterns, irrational beliefs, and cognitive biases (e.g., catastrophizing, black-and-white thinking), can contribute to the maintenance of anxiety symptoms. These cognitive distortions often fuel worries and amplify perceived threats.
- Learned behaviors and coping mechanisms developed in response

to stress or trauma can become maladaptive over time, reinforcing patterns of anxiety and avoidance.

Biological Factors

- Neurobiological abnormalities, including alterations in brain structure and function, may contribute to the development of anxiety disorders. Dysregulation of neural circuits involved in fear processing and emotion regulation, such as the amygdala, prefrontal cortex, and hippocampus, has been implicated in anxiety pathology.
- Imbalances in neurotransmitters, hormonal fluctuations (e.g., cortisol), and dysregulation of the body's stress response system (the hypothalamic-pituitary-adrenal axis) can also play a role in the manifestation of anxiety symptoms.

Overall, anxiety disorders are multifaceted conditions influenced by a combination of genetic, environmental, psychological, and biological factors.

Understanding these underlying causes and triggers is essential for effective diagnosis, treatment, and management of anxiety.

A comprehensive approach that addresses these various factors, such as therapy, medication, lifestyle modifications, and stress management techniques, can help individuals cope with anxiety and improve their quality of life.

The physical, emotional, and cognitive symptoms of anxiety.

Anxiety can manifest in a variety of ways, affecting not only a person's thoughts and emotions but also their physical well-being. Here's a breakdown of the common symptoms of anxiety across *physical, emotional, and cognitive domains*:

Physical Symptoms

- Muscle Tension: Anxiety often leads to muscle tension throughout the body, particularly in the neck, shoulders, and back. This tension can result in stiffness, soreness, and even headaches.
- Increased Heart Rate: When experiencing anxiety, the body's natural response is to increase heart rate in preparation for a perceived threat. This can lead to palpitations or a sensation of a racing heart.
- Shortness of Breath: Anxiety can cause rapid, shallow breathing or the sensation of being unable to take a deep breath. This may lead to hyperventilation, dizziness, or lightheadedness.
- Gastrointestinal Distress: Many people experience digestive issues when anxious, such as nausea, stomach pain, bloating, diarrhea, or constipation. This is due to the body's stress response affecting digestion.
- Sweating: Anxiety often triggers sweating, even in the absence of physical exertion or heat. Palms may become sweaty, and individuals may experience generalized sweating or hot flashes.
- Trembling or Shaking: Anxiety can cause trembling or shaking in the hands, legs, or other parts of the body. This involuntary movement is a result of heightened physiological arousal.
- Fatigue: Chronic anxiety can lead to fatigue and feelings of exhaustion, even after minimal physical or mental exertion. Difficulty falling asleep or staying asleep is also common among individuals with anxiety.

Emotional Symptoms

- <u>Excessive Worry</u>: One of the hallmark emotional symptoms of anxiety is excessive, persistent worry about a wide range of concerns, both real and imagined. Individuals with anxiety may find it difficult to control their worrying thoughts.
- <u>Irritability</u>: Anxiety often manifests as irritability or agitation, leading to a short temper, impatience, or feelings of frustration. This can strain relationships and interpersonal interactions.
- <u>Fear or Panic</u>: Anxiety is characterized by feelings of fear, apprehension, or dread, particularly in response to perceived threats or stressors. In severe cases, anxiety may escalate into panic attacks, which are sudden, intense episodes of fear accompanied by physical symptoms.
- <u>Restlessness</u>: Anxiety can create a sense of restlessness or unease, making it difficult to relax or sit still. Individuals may feel constantly on edge or keyed up, as if anticipating something bad happening.
- <u>Difficulty Concentrating</u>: The cognitive symptoms of anxiety can interfere with concentration, memory, and decision-making. Racing thoughts, mental distractions, and preoccupation with worries may impair cognitive functioning.
- <u>Feelings of Dread or Doom</u>: Individuals with anxiety may experience a pervasive sense of dread or impending doom, even when there's no clear threat. This can lead to feelings of hopelessness or helplessness.

Cognitive Symptoms

- <u>Racing Thoughts</u>: Anxiety often triggers a barrage of racing, intrusive thoughts that are difficult to control or dismiss. These thoughts may be focused on potential threats, worst-case scenarios, or past events.

- <u>Catastrophizing</u>: Individuals with anxiety may engage in catastrophizing, which involves magnifying the severity of potential outcomes or imagining the worst-case scenarios. This cognitive distortion contributes to heightened anxiety and distress.
- <u>Difficulty Relaxing</u>: Anxiety can make it challenging to relax or unwind, as individuals may feel constantly on alert or hypervigilant. Relaxation techniques such as deep breathing or mindfulness may help alleviate this symptom.
- <u>Hypervigilance</u>: Anxiety often leads to hypervigilance, a state of heightened awareness and sensitivity to potential threats or dangers in the environment. This hyperarousal can exacerbate feelings of anxiety and make it difficult to feel safe or at ease.
- <u>Memory Problems</u>: Chronic anxiety can impair memory and cognitive functioning, making it difficult to retain information or recall details accurately. This may contribute to feelings of frustration or inadequacy.

It's important to note that not everyone with anxiety will experience all of these symptoms, and the severity of symptoms can vary widely among individuals. Additionally, anxiety symptoms may overlap with those of other mental health conditions, such as depression or post-traumatic stress disorder (PTSD).

If you or someone you know is experiencing persistent or severe anxiety symptoms, seeking support from a mental health professional is recommended for proper evaluation and treatment.

3

The Mind-Body Connection

he relationship between physical health and mental well-being.

The relationship between physical health and mental well-being is intricate and multifaceted, with each influencing and impacting the other in profound ways. *Here's a deeper exploration of this relationship:*

Biological Mechanisms: The brain and body are interconnected systems, and changes in one can affect the other. For example, neurotransmitters such as serotonin, dopamine, and norepinephrine play crucial roles in both mood regulation and physical health. Imbalances in these neurotransmitters can contribute to both mental health disorders like depression and physical conditions like chronic pain or fatigue.

Stress Response: The body's stress response system, known as the fight-or-flight response, involves the release of stress hormones such as cortisol and adrenaline. While this response is adaptive in the short term, chronic stress can dysregulate the stress response system, leading to increased inflammation, immune system suppression, and a higher risk of physical health problems like cardiovascular disease, diabetes, and gastrointestinal issues. Moreover, chronic stress is a significant risk factor for the development and exacerbation of mental health conditions such as anxiety and depression.

Lifestyle Factors: Health behaviors such as diet, exercise, sleep, and substance use play crucial roles in both physical health and mental well-being. Regular physical activity, for instance, has been shown to improve mood, reduce symptoms of depression and anxiety, and enhance cognitive function. Similarly, a balanced diet rich in nutrients can support brain health and improve mood stability. Conversely, unhealthy lifestyle habits like poor nutrition, sedentary behavior, substance abuse, and inadequate sleep can increase the risk of both physical and mental health problems.

Psychosocial Factors: Social relationships, socioeconomic status, and environmental factors also influence both physical health and mental well-being. Strong social support networks can buffer against stress, promote resilience, and foster a sense of belonging and connectedness, all of which are essential for mental health. Conversely, social isolation, loneliness, discrimination, and adverse childhood experiences can increase the risk of mental health disorders and contribute to physical health disparities.

Integrated Care Approach: Recognizing the interconnectedness of physical and mental health, there has been a growing emphasis on integrated care models that address both aspects holistically. Integrated care involves collaboration between primary care providers, mental health professionals, and other specialists to address the comprehensive needs of individuals with both physical and mental health conditions.

This approach acknowledges that treating physical health problems alone may not fully address the underlying mental health issues and vice versa.

Overall, the relationship between physical health and mental well-being is bidirectional and complex, influenced by biological, psychological, social, and environmental factors. Promoting holistic health and well-being requires addressing the interplay between physical and mental health and adopting integrated approaches that consider the whole person.

By prioritizing both physical and mental health, individuals can achieve greater resilience, vitality, and overall quality of life.

Techniques such as mindfulness, meditation, and deep breathing exercises to calm the mind and reduce anxiety.

Techniques such as mindfulness, meditation, and deep breathing exercises are powerful tools for calming the mind, reducing anxiety, and promoting overall well-being. *Here's an introduction to each:*

Mindfulness: Mindfulness involves paying attention to the present moment with openness, curiosity, and acceptance, without judgment. It's about cultivating awareness of your thoughts, feelings, bodily sensations, and the surrounding environment. Mindfulness practices can help you become more attuned to your internal experiences and develop a greater sense of clarity and perspective. *Here are some mindfulness techniques you can try:*

- <u>Mindful Breathing</u>: Focus your attention on your breath as you inhale and exhale naturally. Notice the sensations of the breath as it enters and leaves your body, without trying to change it. If your mind wanders, gently guide your attention back to the breath.

- Body Scan: Take a few moments to systematically scan through different parts of your body, starting from your toes and gradually moving up to your head. Notice any sensations, tension, or areas of discomfort, and allow yourself to relax and release any tension you may be holding.
- Mindful Walking: Practice walking mindfully by paying attention to each step you take, the sensations of your feet touching the ground, and the movement of your body. Notice the sights, sounds, and smells around you as you walk, staying present in the moment.

Meditation: Meditation involves training the mind to focus and redirect attention, often through the repetition of a specific focus point or mantra. Meditation practices can help cultivate a sense of inner peace, resilience, and emotional balance. *Here are some meditation techniques you can explore:*

- Guided Meditation: Follow along with a guided meditation recording or app that provides instructions and prompts for relaxation, mindfulness, or visualization. This can be especially helpful for beginners or those who prefer structured guidance.
- Breath Awareness Meditation: Similar to mindful breathing, breath awareness meditation involves focusing on the breath as a point of concentration. You can count your breaths, observe the sensations of breathing, or repeat a calming phrase with each breath.
- Loving-Kindness Meditation: This practice involves cultivating feelings of compassion, love, and goodwill towards oneself and others. You can silently repeat phrases such as "May I be happy, may I be healthy, may I be at peace," extending these wishes to

yourself, loved ones, and all beings.

Deep Breathing Exercises: Deep breathing exercises help activate the body's relaxation response, reducing stress and anxiety. They involve breathing deeply and slowly, focusing on the breath to calm the mind and promote relaxation. *Here are a few deep breathing techniques you can try:*

- Diaphragmatic Breathing: Sit or lie down in a comfortable position. Place one hand on your abdomen and the other on your chest. Inhale deeply through your nose, allowing your abdomen to rise as you fill your lungs with air. Exhale slowly through your mouth, feeling your abdomen fall. Repeat for several breaths, focusing on the rhythm of your breath.
- 4-7-8 Breathing: Inhale deeply through your nose for a count of 4 seconds. Hold your breath for a count of 7 seconds. Exhale slowly through your mouth for a count of 8 seconds. Repeat this cycle for several rounds, allowing each breath to be slow, deep, and relaxed.
- Box Breathing: Inhale deeply through your nose for a count of 4 seconds. Hold your breath for a count of 4 seconds. Exhale slowly through your mouth for a count of 4 seconds. Hold your breath for a count of 4 seconds. Repeat this cycle for several rounds, visualizing a box shape with each breath.

These techniques can be practiced individually or combined to create a personalized mindfulness and relaxation practice that suits your preferences and needs.

Consistent practice over time can help cultivate greater calmness, resilience, and emotional well-being, reducing the impact of anxiety on your life.

The importance of nutrition, exercise, and sleep in managing anxiety symptoms.

Nutrition, exercise, and sleep play vital roles in managing anxiety symptoms and promoting overall mental health and well-being. *Here's a discussion on the importance of each:*

Nutrition

- <u>Balanced Diet</u>: Eating a balanced diet rich in nutrients is essential for supporting brain health and regulating mood. Consuming a variety of whole foods, including fruits, vegetables, whole grains, lean proteins, and healthy fats, provides the body with the necessary vitamins, minerals, and antioxidants to function optimally.
- <u>Blood Sugar Regulation</u>: Avoiding large fluctuations in blood sugar levels is important for stabilizing mood and energy levels. Consuming regular, balanced meals and snacks that include complex carbohydrates, protein, and healthy fats can help maintain steady blood sugar levels throughout the day.
- <u>Gut Health</u>: The gut-brain connection, known as the gut microbiome, plays a crucial role in regulating mood and emotional well-being. Eating a diet rich in fiber and fermented foods supports a healthy gut microbiome, which in turn may reduce inflammation and improve mental health.
- <u>Hydration</u>: Staying hydrated is essential for overall health and well-being, including cognitive function and mood regulation. Aim to drink plenty of water throughout the day to maintain hydration levels and support optimal brain function.

Exercise

- <u>Stress Reduction</u>: Regular physical activity is one of the most effective ways to reduce stress and anxiety. Exercise helps release endorphins, the body's natural feel-good chemicals, which can improve mood and promote relaxation.
- <u>Neurotransmitter Regulation</u>: Exercise has been shown to increase levels of neurotransmitters such as serotonin and dopamine, which play key roles in regulating mood and emotions. This can help alleviate symptoms of anxiety and depression.
- <u>Sleep Quality</u>: Engaging in regular exercise can improve sleep quality and duration, which is important for managing anxiety symptoms. However, it's essential to avoid vigorous exercise close to bedtime, as it may interfere with sleep.

Sleep

- <u>Restoration and Repair</u>: Sleep is crucial for the body to repair and regenerate cells, consolidate memories, and process emotions. Chronic sleep deprivation can impair cognitive function, mood regulation, and stress resilience, increasing the risk of anxiety and other mental health problems.
- <u>Stress Reduction</u>: Adequate sleep helps regulate the body's stress response system, reducing levels of stress hormones like cortisol and promoting relaxation. Getting enough sleep can improve mood stability and resilience to stressors.
- <u>Sleep Hygiene</u>: Practicing good sleep hygiene habits, such as maintaining a consistent sleep schedule, creating a relaxing bedtime routine, and creating a comfortable sleep environment, can help improve sleep quality and reduce anxiety symptoms.

In summary, nutrition, exercise, and sleep are foundational pillars of mental health and play integral roles in managing anxiety symptoms.

By prioritizing a balanced diet, regular physical activity, and adequate sleep, individuals can support their overall well-being and reduce the impact of anxiety on their lives.

Additionally, incorporating mindfulness practices, stress management techniques, and seeking support from mental health professionals can further enhance anxiety management and promote resilience.

4

Cognitive Behavioral Techniques

*C**ognitive-behavioral therapy (CBT) and its effectiveness in treating anxiety.***

Cognitive-behavioral therapy (CBT) is a widely recognized and highly effective form of psychotherapy for treating anxiety disorders. It is based on the premise that our thoughts, emotions, and behaviors are interconnected, and by identifying and changing maladaptive thought patterns and behaviors, individuals can alleviate anxiety symptoms and improve their overall quality of life. *Here's an introduction to CBT and its effectiveness in treating anxiety:*

Core Principles of CBT

- Cognitive Restructuring: CBT focuses on identifying and challenging irrational or negative thought patterns that contribute to anxiety. Through cognitive restructuring techniques, individuals learn to recognize and reframe distorted thoughts, replacing them with more realistic and adaptive beliefs.

- <u>Exposure Therapy</u>: Exposure therapy is a key component of CBT for anxiety disorders, particularly phobias and obsessive-compulsive disorder (OCD). It involves gradually exposing individuals to feared situations or stimuli in a controlled and systematic manner, allowing them to confront and overcome their fears.
- <u>Behavioral Activation</u>: CBT emphasizes the importance of behavioral changes in reducing anxiety symptoms. By engaging in activities that bring a sense of pleasure, accomplishment, or mastery, individuals can counteract feelings of avoidance and withdrawal associated with anxiety.
- <u>Skill Building</u>: CBT teaches practical skills and coping strategies for managing anxiety symptoms, including relaxation techniques, problem-solving skills, assertiveness training, and effective communication.

Effectiveness in Treating Anxiety

- <u>Empirical Support</u>: CBT has been extensively researched and has consistently demonstrated efficacy in treating various anxiety disorders, including generalized anxiety disorder (GAD), social anxiety disorder, panic disorder, specific phobias, and OCD. Numerous randomized controlled trials and meta-analyses have shown that CBT is superior to placebo and comparable to medication in reducing anxiety symptoms and preventing relapse.
- <u>Long-Term Benefits</u>: CBT not only reduces anxiety symptoms in the short term but also provides long-term benefits and lower rates of relapse compared to medication alone. By addressing underlying cognitive and behavioral patterns, CBT equips individuals with skills and strategies to manage anxiety more effectively even after therapy has ended.
- <u>Customization and Flexibility</u>: CBT is highly customizable and

can be tailored to meet the unique needs and preferences of each individual. Therapists work collaboratively with clients to identify specific anxiety triggers, set personalized goals, and develop targeted interventions that address their concerns.

- <u>Complementary Approach</u>: CBT can be used as a standalone treatment for anxiety disorders or in combination with medication, depending on the severity of symptoms and individual preferences. For many individuals, a combination of CBT and medication yields the best outcomes, addressing both the psychological and biological aspects of anxiety.

In summary, CBT is a highly effective and evidence-based approach for treating anxiety disorders. By targeting maladaptive thought patterns and behaviors, CBT empowers individuals to overcome anxiety, regain control over their lives, and build resilience to future stressors.

If you're struggling with anxiety, consider seeking support from a qualified mental health professional trained in CBT to explore how this approach can help you.

How to identify and challenge negative thought patterns and beliefs.

Identifying and challenging negative thought patterns and beliefs is a key component of cognitive-behavioral therapy (CBT), a widely used approach for treating anxiety and other mental health issues. *Here's a step-by-step guide to help readers recognize and reframe their negative thinking:*

Recognize Negative Thoughts

- Pay attention to your thoughts and notice when you're feeling anxious, upset, or stressed.
- Identify the specific thoughts that are contributing to your negative emotions. These thoughts are often automatic and may be distorted or irrational.

Challenge Negative Thoughts

- Reality Testing: Ask yourself if there is evidence to support your negative thoughts. Are they based on facts or assumptions?
- Alternative Perspectives: Consider alternative explanations or viewpoints. How would someone else interpret the situation?
- Worst-Case Scenario: Evaluate the likelihood and consequences of your feared outcomes. Is there a more realistic or less catastrophic outcome?
- Decatastrophizing: Challenge catastrophic thinking by considering more balanced or neutral interpretations of events. What's the worst that could happen, and how could you cope if it did?

Reframe Negative Thoughts

- Positive Reframing: Reframe negative thoughts into more positive or neutral statements. For example, instead of "I'm a failure," reframe it as "I may have made a mistake, but that doesn't define my worth."
- Balanced Thinking: Strive for balanced thinking by considering both the positives and negatives of a situation. Avoid all-or-nothing thinking (e.g., "I always mess up") and focus on the nuances.
- Compassionate Self-Talk: Practice self-compassion by speaking to yourself as you would to a friend. Be kind and understanding, rather than harsh and critical.

Practice Thought Records

- Keep a thought diary to track your negative thoughts, the situations that trigger them, and your emotional responses.
- Use a thought record worksheet to challenge and reframe your negative thoughts systematically. Write down the negative thought, the evidence for and against it, and a more balanced or realistic alternative thought.

Challenge Cognitive Distortions

- Learn to recognize common cognitive distortions, such as all-or-nothing thinking, catastrophizing, overgeneralization, and personalization.
- When you identify these distortions in your thinking, challenge them using the techniques mentioned above. Ask yourself if there's a more realistic or balanced way to interpret the situation.

Practice Mindfulness

- Mindfulness can help you become more aware of your thoughts and emotions without judgment. It can also help you distance yourself from your negative thoughts and see them more objectively.
- Incorporate mindfulness practices, such as mindful breathing or body scan meditation, into your daily routine to enhance your ability to challenge negative thoughts.

By learning to identify and challenge negative thought patterns and beliefs, you can develop a more balanced and realistic perspective, reduce anxiety, and improve your overall mental well-being.

Regular practice of these techniques can help you cultivate a more positive and adaptive mindset, leading to greater resilience and emotional health.

Short exercises for practicing cognitive restructuring and reframing techniques.

Here are some short exercises for practicing cognitive restructuring and reframing techniques:

Evidence-Based Thinking

1. Identify a negative thought you're experiencing, such as "I'm going to fail this exam."
2. Challenge this thought by asking yourself for evidence to support and refute it. For example:
3. Evidence supporting the thought: "I haven't studied enough, and I've struggled with similar tests in the past."
4. Evidence refuting the thought: "I've prepared as best as I could, and I've been improving in this subject over time."
5. Write down the evidence for and against the negative thought, and then reframe it into a more balanced statement. For example: "While I may feel nervous about the exam, I've put in effort to prepare, and I'm capable of handling challenges."

Alternative Interpretations

1. Think of a recent situation that triggered a negative emotion, such as feeling rejected after not receiving an invitation to a social event.

2. Identify the automatic negative thought associated with the situation, such as "Nobody likes me."
3. Generate alternative interpretations or explanations for the situation.

For example:

1. "Perhaps the event was small, and not everyone could be invited."
2. "Maybe the host didn't realize I would be interested in attending."
3. "It's possible that my friend simply forgot to extend the invitation."

Choose one or more alternative interpretations that feel more plausible or balanced, and challenge the original negative thought.

Worst-Case Scenario vs. Realistic Outcome

1. Imagine a situation you're worried about, such as giving a presentation at work.
2. Identify the worst-case scenario that's fueling your anxiety, such as "I'll embarrass myself in front of everyone."
3. Consider the likelihood of this worst-case scenario happening and its potential consequences. Then, challenge it by imagining a more realistic outcome.
4. Reframe the negative thought by acknowledging the possibility of challenges or mistakes while also recognizing your ability to handle them. For example: "While it's possible that I might make a mistake during the presentation, I'm prepared and capable of handling any unexpected situations that arise."

Positive Affirmations

1. Choose a positive affirmation or mantra that resonates with you, such as "I am capable and resilient" or "I deserve happiness and success."
2. Repeat this affirmation to yourself several times throughout the day, especially when you notice negative thoughts creeping in.
3. Visualize yourself embodying the qualities or beliefs expressed in the affirmation, and allow yourself to feel the emotions associated with it.
4. Use the affirmation as a tool to counteract negative self-talk and cultivate a more positive and empowering mindset.

These exercises are designed to help you practice cognitive restructuring and reframing techniques in a structured and accessible way. With regular practice, you can gradually shift your thinking patterns towards greater balance, resilience, and well-being.

5

Stress Management Strategies

he impact of stress on anxiety and vice versa.

Stress and anxiety are closely interconnected, with each often exacerbating the other in a vicious cycle that can significantly impact mental and physical well-being. *Here's a discussion on the impact of stress on anxiety and vice versa:*

Impact of Stress on Anxiety

- Heightened Arousal: Stress activates the body's fight-or-flight response, triggering the release of stress hormones such as cortisol and adrenaline. This heightened physiological arousal can exacerbate symptoms of anxiety, leading to increased feelings of worry, agitation, and nervousness.
- Cognitive Overload: Chronic stress can overwhelm the mind with incessant worries and concerns, making it difficult to think clearly or rationally. This cognitive overload can contribute to the development or exacerbation of anxiety disorders such as

generalized anxiety disorder (GAD) or panic disorder.

- Hypervigilance: Stress can heighten vigilance and sensitivity to potential threats, leading to increased anxiety and perceived danger in everyday situations. Individuals may become hyperaware of potential stressors, leading to a state of hypervigilance and persistent anxiety.

- Disruption of Coping Mechanisms: Chronic stress can deplete coping resources and undermine resilience, making it harder to cope with everyday stressors and challenges. This can create a sense of helplessness and vulnerability, further fueling anxiety symptoms.

- Increased Risk of Anxiety Disorders: Prolonged exposure to stress is a significant risk factor for the development of anxiety disorders. Chronic stress can dysregulate the body's stress response system, leading to structural and functional changes in the brain that predispose individuals to anxiety disorders.

Impact of Anxiety on Stress

- Magnification of Stressors: Anxiety can magnify the perceived severity of stressors and challenges, making them seem more overwhelming and insurmountable. Individuals with anxiety may catastrophize potential outcomes and anticipate the worst-case scenarios, leading to increased stress levels.

- Heightened Physiological Response: Anxiety triggers a physiological stress response similar to that of acute stress, leading to increased heart rate, rapid breathing, muscle tension, and other physical symptoms associated with stress. This heightened physiological arousal can exacerbate the body's response to stressors, amplifying stress levels.

- Impaired Coping Abilities: Anxiety can impair coping abilities and problem-solving skills, making it harder to effectively manage stressors and adapt to changing circumstances. Individuals may resort to avoidance or maladaptive coping mechanisms, which can further exacerbate stress and perpetuate the cycle of anxiety.

- <u>Interference with Relaxation</u>: Anxiety can interfere with relaxation and recovery from stress by maintaining a state of heightened arousal and vigilance. Individuals may struggle to unwind and experience restful sleep, leading to persistent feelings of tension and fatigue.
- <u>Chronic Activation of Stress Response</u>: Prolonged anxiety can chronically activate the body's stress response system, leading to wear and tear on the body and increasing vulnerability to stress-related health problems such as cardiovascular disease, immune dysfunction, and gastrointestinal disorders.

In summary, stress and anxiety are intimately linked, each influencing and amplifying the other in a complex interplay that can have profound effects on mental and physical health.

Breaking the cycle of stress and anxiety often requires comprehensive interventions that address both the underlying stressors and the maladaptive thought patterns and behaviors associated with anxiety.

By learning effective coping strategies, practicing stress management techniques, and seeking support from mental health professionals, individuals can reduce the impact of stress and anxiety on their lives and cultivate greater resilience and well-being.

Practical tips for managing stressors in daily life, such as time management, setting boundaries, and practicing self-care.

Managing stressors in daily life involves adopting practical strategies to cope with challenges, prioritize tasks, and nurture your well-being. *Here are some tips for managing stressors effectively:*

Prioritize Tasks

- Make a to-do list or use a planner to prioritize tasks based on urgency and importance.
- Break larger tasks into smaller, manageable steps to avoid feeling overwhelmed.
- Focus on completing one task at a time rather than trying to multitask, which can increase stress and reduce productivity.

Practice Time Management

- Set realistic goals and deadlines for completing tasks, taking into account your energy levels and available resources.
- Use time-blocking techniques to allocate specific time slots for different activities, including work, relaxation, exercise, and socializing.
- Limit distractions by turning off notifications, setting boundaries around work hours, and creating a dedicated workspace free from interruptions.

Set Boundaries

- Learn to say no to requests or commitments that exceed your capacity or compromise your well-being.
- Communicate your boundaries assertively and respectfully, expressing your needs and limitations to others.
- Prioritize self-care and allocate time for rest, relaxation, and

activities that replenish your energy and nurture your mental health.

Practice Stress Management Techniques

- Incorporate stress-reduction techniques into your daily routine, such as deep breathing exercises, mindfulness meditation, progressive muscle relaxation, or guided imagery.
- Take short breaks throughout the day to stretch, walk, or engage in activities that help you relax and recharge.
- Engage in physical activity regularly, such as walking, jogging, yoga, or dancing, to release tension and boost mood.

Cultivate Supportive Relationships

- Seek social support from friends, family members, or support groups who can provide encouragement, empathy, and practical assistance during stressful times.
- Nurture positive relationships and prioritize spending time with loved ones who uplift and energize you.
- Practice active listening and empathy when supporting others, fostering reciprocal relationships based on mutual respect and understanding.

Practice Self-Care

- Prioritize self-care activities that promote physical, emotional, and mental well-being, such as adequate sleep, nutritious eating, regular exercise, and relaxation techniques.
- Engage in hobbies and activities that bring you joy, fulfillment, and a sense of purpose.

- Set aside time for activities that replenish your energy and nourish your soul, whether it's reading, gardening, listening to music, or spending time in nature.

Seek Professional Support

- If stressors become overwhelming or persist despite your efforts to manage them, consider seeking support from a mental health professional.
- Therapy can provide tools, strategies, and coping skills to navigate stressors more effectively and build resilience in the face of adversity.
- Don't hesitate to reach out for help if you're struggling with stress, anxiety, or other mental health concerns. You don't have to face challenges alone.

By incorporating these practical tips into your daily life, you can better manage stressors, enhance your resilience, and cultivate a greater sense of balance, well-being, and fulfillment.

Remember that managing stress is an ongoing process, and it's essential to prioritize self-care and seek support when needed.

Relaxation techniques like progressive muscle relaxation and visualization.

Relaxation techniques are powerful tools for reducing stress, promoting calmness, and enhancing overall well-being. Two commonly used relaxation techniques are progressive muscle relaxation and visualization.

Here's an introduction to each:

Progressive Muscle Relaxation (PMR)

- Progressive muscle relaxation is a systematic technique that involves tensing and then relaxing different muscle groups in the body to release physical tension and promote relaxation.
- Start by finding a quiet and comfortable place to sit or lie down. Close your eyes and take a few deep breaths to center yourself.
- Begin with a specific muscle group, such as your hands or feet. Tense the muscles in that group as tightly as you can, holding the tension for a few seconds.
- Then, slowly release the tension while focusing on the sensation of relaxation spreading through the muscle group. Pay attention to the difference between tension and relaxation.
- Continue this process, moving through each muscle group in your body, from your feet to your head. Progressively tense and relax each muscle group, taking your time to fully experience the relaxation.
- As you practice PMR regularly, you'll become more adept at recognizing and releasing tension in your body, promoting deep relaxation and stress relief.

Visualization

- Visualization, also known as guided imagery or mental imagery, involves using your imagination to create vivid mental images or scenarios that promote relaxation, well-being, and positive change.
- Find a comfortable position and close your eyes. Take a few deep breaths to relax your body and clear your mind.
- Visualize yourself in a peaceful and serene setting, such as a tranquil

beach, lush forest, or serene mountaintop. Imagine the sights, sounds, smells, and sensations of being in this place.

- Engage your senses fully as you immerse yourself in the visualization. Notice the warmth of the sun on your skin, the sound of gentle waves lapping against the shore, or the scent of pine trees in the forest.
- Allow yourself to experience feelings of calmness, relaxation, and tranquility as you continue to visualize the scene unfolding in your mind.
- You can also incorporate positive affirmations or intentions into your visualization, such as repeating statements like "I am calm and at peace" or "I am surrounded by love and light."

Both progressive muscle relaxation and visualization can be practiced independently or combined with other relaxation techniques, such as deep breathing or mindfulness meditation, to enhance their effectiveness.

Experiment with different techniques to find what works best for you, and incorporate relaxation practices into your daily routine to promote greater relaxation, stress relief, and overall well-being.

6

Building Resilience

*T**he concept of resilience and its role in coping with anxiety.*

Resilience is the ability to adapt and bounce back in the face of adversity, trauma, or significant stress. It involves harnessing inner strengths, coping mechanisms, and support systems to navigate challenges, maintain emotional well-being, and thrive despite difficult circumstances. Resilience plays a crucial role in coping with anxiety by helping individuals manage stressors more effectively, cultivate a positive mindset, and build greater emotional and psychological strength. *Here's how resilience contributes to coping with anxiety:*

Emotional Regulation: Resilient individuals are better equipped to regulate their emotions and cope with distressing feelings associated with anxiety. They can recognize and acknowledge their emotions without becoming overwhelmed by them, allowing them to respond to stressors in a more balanced and adaptive manner.

Flexible Thinking: Resilience involves having a flexible and adaptable mindset that allows for creative problem-solving and perspective-taking. When faced with anxiety-provoking situations, resilient individuals can reframe challenges as opportunities for growth, learning, and personal development, rather than insurmountable obstacles.

Effective Coping Strategies: Resilient individuals possess a repertoire of effective coping strategies and resources that help them navigate stressful situations. They may engage in problem-focused coping (taking action to address the source of stress) and emotion-focused coping (managing emotional distress), drawing upon social support, self-care practices, and relaxation techniques to manage anxiety symptoms.

Optimism and Hope: Resilience is characterized by a sense of optimism, hope, and belief in one's ability to overcome difficulties. Resilient individuals maintain a positive outlook on life, viewing setbacks and failures as temporary and surmountable. This optimistic mindset serves as a protective factor against anxiety and fosters resilience in the face of adversity.

Social Support Networks: Resilient individuals tend to have strong social support networks comprised of friends, family members, mentors, and other sources of support. These connections provide emotional validation, encouragement, and practical assistance during times of stress, buffering against the negative effects of anxiety and promoting resilience.

Self-Efficacy and Confidence: Resilience is closely linked to self-efficacy—the belief in one's ability to achieve goals and overcome challenges. Resilient individuals have a strong sense of self-efficacy and confidence in their capacity to cope with stressors, which empowers them to take proactive steps to manage anxiety and navigate adversity effectively.

Meaning and Purpose: Resilient individuals often derive a sense of meaning and purpose from their experiences, values, and goals. They are motivated by a sense of purpose and direction in life, which provides resilience in the face of anxiety-provoking situations and helps them maintain perspective and resilience.

Overall, resilience is a dynamic process that can be cultivated and strengthened over time through self-awareness, coping skills development, and supportive relationships.

By fostering resilience, individuals can enhance their ability to cope with anxiety, overcome challenges, and thrive in the face of adversity.

Strategies for cultivating resilience, including developing a support network, fostering optimism, and embracing change.

Cultivating resilience involves developing skills, mindset, and support systems that help individuals navigate challenges, bounce back from setbacks, and thrive in the face of adversity. *Here are some strategies for cultivating resilience:*

Developing a Support Network

- Foster strong connections with friends, family members, colleagues, mentors, and other supportive individuals who provide emotional validation, encouragement, and practical assistance during difficult times.
- Seek out community groups, support networks, or therapy groups

where you can connect with others who share similar experiences and provide mutual support.

- Don't hesitate to reach out for help when needed. Sharing your struggles with trusted individuals can alleviate feelings of isolation and provide perspective and guidance.

Fostering Optimism

- Cultivate a positive mindset by focusing on opportunities for growth, learning, and personal development, even in the face of adversity.
- Practice gratitude by reflecting on the things you're thankful for each day, no matter how small. Gratitude can shift your focus from what's lacking to what's present and meaningful in your life.
- Challenge negative thinking patterns and cultivate self-compassion by reframing setbacks as temporary and surmountable, rather than permanent and insurmountable.

Embracing Change

- Develop adaptability and flexibility by embracing change as a natural part of life. Recognize that change can lead to growth, new opportunities, and personal transformation.
- Practice mindfulness and acceptance to cultivate a nonjudgmental awareness of the present moment, allowing you to respond to change with greater clarity, composure, and resilience.
- Focus on what you can control and influence, rather than dwelling on factors beyond your control. Channel your energy into taking proactive steps to adapt to change and navigate uncertainty effectively.

Building Coping Skills

- Develop a toolkit of coping skills and strategies to manage stress, anxiety, and other challenges. This may include relaxation techniques (e.g., deep breathing, meditation, progressive muscle relaxation), problem-solving skills, assertiveness training, and effective communication.
- Practice self-care regularly by prioritizing activities that nourish your physical, emotional, and mental well-being. This may include exercise, healthy eating, adequate sleep, hobbies, creative expression, and time spent in nature.

Setting Realistic Goals

- Set realistic and achievable goals that align with your values, interests, and aspirations. Break larger goals into smaller, manageable steps to maintain motivation and momentum.
- Celebrate your progress and accomplishments along the way, recognizing the effort and resilience required to pursue your goals despite obstacles and setbacks.

Cultivating Meaning and Purpose

- Identify your core values, passions, and strengths, and seek opportunities to align your actions with these values. Engage in activities that bring meaning and purpose to your life, whether it's volunteering, pursuing creative endeavors, or helping others in need.
- Find meaning in difficult experiences by reflecting on what you've learned, how you've grown, and how you can use your experiences to contribute to your own growth and the well-being of others.

By incorporating these strategies into your daily life, you can cultivate resilience and strengthen your ability to cope with adversity, navigate challenges, and thrive in the face of uncertainty.

Remember that resilience is a dynamic process that evolves over time, and by fostering resilience, you can build greater capacity to bounce back from setbacks and live a more fulfilling and resilient life.

7

Lifestyle Changes

T*he importance of making lifestyle changes to support mental health.*

Making lifestyle changes to support mental health is crucial for promoting overall well-being, resilience, and emotional balance. Lifestyle factors such as diet, exercise, sleep, stress management, social connections, and leisure activities play integral roles in shaping mental health outcomes. *Here's why making these changes is important:*

Physical Health and Mental Well-Being Connection

- Physical health and mental health are closely intertwined. Lifestyle factors that promote physical health, such as regular exercise, nutritious eating, and adequate sleep, also have positive effects on mental well-being.
- Engaging in regular physical activity releases endorphins, neurotransmitters that promote feelings of happiness and reduce stress. Similarly, a balanced diet provides essential nutrients that support

brain function and mood regulation.

- Prioritizing sleep hygiene and getting sufficient restorative sleep is essential for cognitive function, emotional regulation, and stress resilience.

Stress Management and Resilience

- Lifestyle changes that promote stress management and resilience are key for maintaining mental health in the face of challenges and adversity.
- Engaging in relaxation techniques such as deep breathing, mindfulness meditation, or progressive muscle relaxation can help reduce stress levels and promote relaxation.
- Building resilience through coping skills development, problem-solving strategies, and social support networks enhances the ability to navigate stressors effectively and bounce back from setbacks.

Social Connections and Support

- Strong social connections and supportive relationships are protective factors for mental health. Maintaining meaningful social connections and seeking support from friends, family, or support groups can buffer against the negative effects of stress and adversity.
- Prioritizing quality time with loved ones, engaging in activities with others, and fostering a sense of belonging and community can enhance emotional well-being and provide valuable support during challenging times.

Healthy Coping Mechanisms

- Lifestyle changes promote the adoption of healthy coping mechanisms and self-care practices that support mental health. This may include engaging in hobbies, creative expression, relaxation activities, or spending time in nature.

- Avoiding maladaptive coping mechanisms such as substance abuse, excessive screen time, or avoidance behaviors is essential for preserving mental health and well-being.

Preventive Mental Health Care

- Making proactive lifestyle changes can serve as preventive mental health care, reducing the risk of developing mental health problems and promoting resilience and emotional well-being.
- By prioritizing self-care, stress management, and healthy coping strategies, individuals can take proactive steps to protect their mental health and reduce the likelihood of experiencing mental health challenges in the future.

In summary, making lifestyle changes to support mental health is essential for promoting resilience, emotional well-being, and overall quality of life.

By prioritizing physical health, stress management, social connections, and healthy coping mechanisms, individuals can cultivate a strong foundation for mental health and thrive in all aspects of their lives.

Creating a healthy work-life balance, setting realistic goals, and prioritizing self-care activities.

Creating a healthy work-life balance, setting realistic goals, and prioritizing self-care activities are essential for maintaining well-being, reducing stress, and enhancing overall quality of life. *Here's some advice on how to achieve these important aspects of self-care:*

Creating a Healthy Work-Life Balance

- <u>Set boundaries</u>: Establish clear boundaries between work and personal life by defining specific work hours and sticking to them as much as possible. Avoid checking work emails or taking calls during non-work hours.
- <u>Prioritize tasks</u>: Identify the most important tasks at work and focus on completing them efficiently. Learn to delegate tasks when necessary and avoid overcommitting yourself.
- <u>Schedule downtime</u>: Set aside time each day for leisure activities, hobbies, and relaxation. Schedule regular breaks throughout the day to recharge and prevent burnout.
- <u>Unplug regularly</u>: Take regular breaks from technology and screens to reduce mental fatigue and promote relaxation. Engage in activities that don't involve screens, such as reading, spending time outdoors, or practicing mindfulness.

Setting Realistic Goals

- <u>Break goals into smaller steps</u>: Divide larger goals into smaller, manageable tasks to avoid feeling overwhelmed. Focus on making progress one step at a time, celebrating achievements along the way.
- <u>Be specific and measurable</u>: Set clear, specific goals that are measurable and achievable within a reasonable timeframe. Define what success looks like and track your progress regularly.
- <u>Adjust as needed</u>: Be flexible and willing to adjust your goals as circumstances change. If you encounter obstacles or setbacks,

reassess your goals and make necessary adjustments to stay on track.

- Focus on priorities: Identify your top priorities and allocate time and resources accordingly. Let go of goals that are no longer relevant or aligned with your values and aspirations.

Prioritizing Self-Care Activities

- Make self-care a priority: Recognize the importance of self-care for your physical, emotional, and mental well-being. Prioritize self-care activities just as you would any other important commitment.
- Schedule self-care time: Block out time in your schedule for self-care activities, whether it's exercise, meditation, journaling, or spending time with loved ones. Treat self-care as non-negotiable time for yourself.
- Choose activities that nourish you: Identify self-care activities that replenish your energy and bring you joy, whether it's going for a walk, taking a bubble bath, or practicing a hobby you love.
- Practice self-compassion: Be kind and compassionate toward yourself, especially during times of stress or difficulty. Acknowledge your efforts and accomplishments, and treat yourself with the same care and compassion you would offer to a friend.

By implementing these strategies, you can cultivate a healthier work-life balance, set realistic goals, and prioritize self-care activities that support your overall well-being and happiness.

Remember that self-care is not selfish—it's an essential part of maintaining your physical, emotional, and mental health in the long run.

Tips for managing relationships and social interactions while coping with anxiety.

Managing relationships and social interactions while coping with anxiety can present unique challenges, but with the right strategies and support, it's possible to navigate these situations more effectively. *Here are some tips for managing relationships and social interactions while coping with anxiety:*

Communicate Openly

- Be open and honest with trusted friends, family members, or partners about your anxiety. Communicate your needs, boundaries, and preferences in social situations, such as the need for reassurance, understanding, or accommodation.
- Share specific ways that others can support you, whether it's offering encouragement, listening without judgment, or helping you navigate social events.

Set Boundaries

- Set clear boundaries around social interactions to protect your mental health and well-being. Recognize when you need to step back from social activities or prioritize self-care, and communicate your boundaries assertively and respectfully.
- Don't feel obligated to attend every social event or engage in activities that exacerbate your anxiety. It's okay to decline invitations or take breaks when needed to prioritize your mental health.

Practice Self-Compassion

- Be kind and compassionate toward yourself, especially when facing social anxiety triggers or challenging social situations. Acknowledge your feelings without judgment and remind yourself that it's okay to feel anxious at times.
- Practice self-soothing techniques, such as deep breathing, positive self-talk, or grounding exercises, to calm your nerves and regulate your emotions in social settings.

Focus on Quality Over Quantity

- Prioritize meaningful connections with a few close friends or supportive individuals who understand and accept you, rather than trying to maintain a large social circle.
- Invest time and energy in nurturing relationships that bring you joy, fulfillment, and support. Surround yourself with people who uplift and empower you, rather than drain your energy or exacerbate your anxiety.

Take Small Steps

- Gradually expose yourself to social situations that trigger anxiety, starting with smaller, less intimidating settings and gradually working your way up to more challenging situations.
- Break social interactions into manageable steps, such as attending a social event for a short time or initiating a conversation with one person at a time. Celebrate your progress and achievements, no matter how small.

Practice Mindfulness

- Use mindfulness techniques to stay present and grounded in social situations, rather than getting lost in worries or self-critical thoughts. Focus on your breath, senses, or surroundings to anchor yourself in the present moment.

- Notice any anxious thoughts or sensations without judgment and gently redirect your attention back to the present moment. Accept whatever arises with compassion and self-awareness.

Seek Professional Support

- Consider seeking support from a therapist or counselor who specializes in anxiety disorders. Therapy can provide valuable tools, strategies, and support for managing social anxiety and improving interpersonal relationships.
- Cognitive-behavioral therapy (CBT), exposure therapy, and inter-personal therapy are effective approaches for addressing social anxiety and enhancing social skills and confidence.

Remember that managing relationships and social interactions while coping with anxiety is a journey that requires patience, self-awareness, and practice.

Be gentle with yourself as you navigate social challenges, and don't hesitate to reach out for support when needed. With time and effort, you can develop healthier relationships and feel more confident and at ease in social settings.

8

Seeking Professional Help

The stigma surrounding mental health treatment.

Addressing the stigma surrounding mental health treatment is crucial for promoting understanding, empathy, and access to support for individuals experiencing mental health challenges. Stigma refers to negative attitudes, beliefs, and stereotypes that contribute to discrimination and marginalization of individuals with mental health conditions. *Here are some key points to consider when addressing mental health stigma:*

Education and Awareness

- Increase public awareness and understanding of mental health conditions by providing accurate information about the causes, symptoms, and treatments of mental illnesses.
- Challenge common myths and misconceptions about mental health by promoting messages of hope, recovery, and resilience. Encourage open dialogue and honest conversations about mental health

in schools, workplaces, and communities.

Language Matters

- Use language that is respectful, inclusive, and person-centered when discussing mental health. Avoid stigmatizing language or labels that perpetuate stereotypes or reinforce negative attitudes.
- Emphasize the importance of using nonjudgmental language that acknowledges the individual's experiences and humanity, rather than reducing them to their diagnosis or symptoms.

Promote Help-Seeking Behavior

- Encourage individuals to seek help for mental health concerns without fear of judgment or discrimination. Normalize help-seeking behavior by emphasizing that seeking support is a sign of strength, not weakness.
- Provide information about available resources, such as counseling services, support groups, hotlines, and online forums, to help individuals access the support they need.

Combat Discrimination and Stigmatization

- Advocate for policies and initiatives that promote equality, inclusion, and anti-discrimination in mental health care and services. Support legislative efforts to protect the rights of individuals with mental health conditions and ensure equal access to treatment and support.
- Challenge instances of discrimination or stigmatization in society, whether it's in the media, healthcare system, workplace, or community. Speak out against stigma and discrimination when you

encounter it, and promote acceptance and empathy instead.

Lead by Example

- Model compassionate and supportive behavior toward individuals with mental health conditions. Be a source of encouragement, validation, and understanding for those who may be struggling with their mental health.
- Share your own experiences with mental health challenges or treatment to reduce stigma and show others that they are not alone in their struggles. By sharing your story, you can help break down barriers and inspire hope in others.

Promote Cultural Competence

- Recognize and address the intersectionality of mental health stigma with other forms of discrimination, such as racism, sexism, homophobia, or ableism. Promote cultural competence and sensitivity in mental health care to ensure that services are accessible and inclusive for all individuals.
- Respect and validate diverse experiences of mental health within different cultural, ethnic, and social groups. Tailor mental health interventions and services to meet the unique needs and preferences of individuals from diverse backgrounds.

Addressing mental health stigma requires collective efforts from individuals, communities, organizations, and policymakers.

By promoting understanding, empathy, and acceptance, we can create a more supportive and inclusive society where everyone feels valued, respected, and empowered to seek help for their mental health needs.

When and how to seek professional help for anxiety, including therapy, medication, and support groups.

Knowing when and how to seek professional help for anxiety is essential for managing symptoms effectively and improving overall well-being. *Here are some guidelines for seeking professional help for anxiety:*

Recognizing Symptoms

- Pay attention to signs and symptoms of anxiety, such as excessive worry, restlessness, irritability, difficulty concentrating, muscle tension, and sleep disturbances.
- Notice how anxiety affects various areas of your life, including work, relationships, and daily functioning. If anxiety significantly impairs your ability to engage in activities or enjoy life, it may be time to seek professional help.

Assessing Severity

- Consider the severity and duration of your anxiety symptoms. If anxiety persists for several weeks or months and interferes with your ability to function, it may indicate an anxiety disorder that requires professional treatment.
- Assess the impact of anxiety on your quality of life, relationships, and overall well-being. If anxiety causes significant distress or impairment, it's important to seek help from a mental health professional.

Seeking Therapy

- Therapy, such as cognitive-behavioral therapy (CBT), is often recommended as a first-line treatment for anxiety disorders. CBT helps individuals identify and challenge negative thought patterns and develop coping skills to manage anxiety more effectively.
- Consider seeking therapy from a licensed mental health professional, such as a psychologist, counselor, or therapist, who specializes in treating anxiety disorders. Look for someone with experience and expertise in evidence-based treatments for anxiety.
- Therapy can be conducted in individual, group, or family settings, depending on your preferences and needs. Discuss treatment options with your therapist to determine the most appropriate approach for you.

Considering Medication

- In some cases, medication may be prescribed to help manage anxiety symptoms, especially when therapy alone is insufficient or symptoms are severe.
- Talk to your primary care physician or a psychiatrist about medication options for anxiety. They can assess your symptoms, medical history, and treatment preferences to determine whether medication is appropriate for you.
- Medications commonly used to treat anxiety disorders include selective serotonin reuptake inhibitors (SSRIs), serotonin-norepinephrine reuptake inhibitors (SNRIs), benzodiazepines, and other antidepressants. Work closely with your healthcare provider to find the right medication and dosage for your needs.

Joining Support Groups

- Support groups can provide valuable peer support, encouragement, and practical coping strategies for managing anxiety. Consider joining a local or online support group for individuals with anxiety disorders.

- Support groups may be facilitated by mental health professionals or peer-led, depending on the format and focus of the group. Look for groups that align with your needs and preferences, and feel comfortable sharing and connecting with others who understand your experiences.

Making the Decision

- Trust your instincts and intuition when deciding to seek professional help for anxiety. If you're unsure whether your symptoms warrant treatment, consider scheduling an evaluation with a mental health professional to discuss your concerns.
- Remember that seeking help is a sign of strength, not weakness. You deserve support and assistance in managing your anxiety, and there are effective treatments available to help you feel better.

Overall, seeking professional help for anxiety involves recognizing symptoms, assessing severity, and exploring treatment options that align with your needs and preferences. Whether it's therapy, medication, support groups, or a combination of these approaches, taking proactive steps to address anxiety can lead to symptom relief, improved functioning, and enhanced quality of life.

9

Conclusion

The key takeaways from the book

Here are the key takeaways from the book on coping with anxiety:

Understanding Anxiety: Anxiety is a common and normal human experience, but when it becomes excessive or overwhelming, it can interfere with daily functioning and quality of life. Learning to recognize the signs and symptoms of anxiety is the first step toward managing it effectively.

Causes and Triggers: Anxiety can be triggered by a variety of factors, including genetic predisposition, environmental stressors, traumatic experiences, and psychological vulnerabilities. Understanding the underlying causes of anxiety can help individuals develop targeted strategies for coping and treatment.

Physical, Emotional, and Cognitive Symptoms: Anxiety manifests in a variety of ways, including physical symptoms (e.g., rapid heartbeat, muscle tension), emotional symptoms (e.g., excessive worry, irritability), and cognitive symptoms (e.g., racing thoughts, difficulty concentrating). Recognizing these symptoms can help individuals identify when they are experiencing anxiety and take appropriate action.

Holistic Approach to Treatment: Managing anxiety often requires a holistic approach that addresses the physical, emotional, cognitive, and behavioral aspects of the condition. This may include therapy (such as cognitive-behavioral therapy), medication, lifestyle changes, stress management techniques, and social support.

Self-Help Strategies: There are many self-help strategies that individuals can use to cope with anxiety on their own. These may include relaxation techniques (such as deep breathing and mindfulness meditation), cognitive restructuring, lifestyle changes (such as exercise, nutrition, and sleep), setting boundaries, and practicing self-compassion.

Seeking Professional Help: While self-help strategies can be beneficial, it's also important to know when to seek professional help for anxiety. Therapy, medication, and support groups can provide valuable resources and support for individuals struggling with anxiety. It's important to reach out for help when anxiety symptoms are severe, persistent, or significantly impairing daily functioning.

Building Resilience: Cultivating resilience is essential for coping with anxiety and navigating life's challenges. Building resilience involves developing coping skills, fostering social connections, practicing self-care, setting realistic goals, and maintaining a positive outlook. By building resilience, individuals can better manage anxiety and thrive in the face of adversity.

Overall, coping with anxiety requires a multifaceted approach that addresses the underlying causes, symptoms, and triggers of anxiety, while also promoting resilience, self-care, and well-being.

With the right tools, strategies, and support, individuals can learn to manage their anxiety effectively and lead fulfilling lives.

Encouragement and support to you on your journey to managing anxiety.

You are not alone. Anxiety is a common experience that many people face at some point in their lives, and it does not define you. Your struggles with anxiety are valid, and there is hope for healing and growth.

Remember that you are stronger than you think. Every step you take toward managing your anxiety, no matter how small, is a testament to your resilience and courage. Each day, you are making progress, even if it may not always feel that way.

Be kind to yourself. Managing anxiety can be challenging, and it's okay to have setbacks along the way. Treat yourself with the same compassion and understanding that you would offer to a friend facing similar struggles. You are deserving of love, support, and self-care.

Reach out for help when you need it. You do not have to face anxiety alone. Whether it's seeking support from a therapist, confiding in a trusted friend, or joining a support group, there are people who care about you and want to help you through this journey.

Celebrate your victories, no matter how small. Recognize and acknowledge the progress you've made, whether it's trying a new coping strategy, facing a fear, or reaching out for help. Each step forward is a triumph worth celebrating.

Keep moving forward, one day at a time. Remember that healing is a journey, and it's okay to take things one step at a time. Be patient with yourself, and trust that with time, effort, and support, you can learn to manage your anxiety and live a fulfilling life.

You are capable, you are resilient, and you are worthy of peace and happiness. Believe in yourself, and know that brighter days are ahead. You have the strength within you to overcome anxiety and thrive. Keep going—you've got this.

10

Resources

Stiles, K. (2021, July 30). 45 quotes about anxiety. Psych Central. Retrieved April 27, 2024, from https://psychcentral.com/anxiety/quotes-about-anxiety#living-with-anxiety.

ChatGPT. (n.d.). https://chat.openai.com/. Retrieved April 27, 2024, from https://chat.openai.com/.